DREAM OF MAKING AN EGALITARIAN SOCIETY IN BANGLADESH

MD. SAD BIN ABI

DREAM OF MAKING AN EGALITARIAN SOCIETY IN
BANGLADESH

Copyright © 2020 Md. Sad Bin Abi

All rights reserved.

ISBN: 9798653614651

DEDICATION

This book is dedicated to the people of this world who are fortunately or unfortunately can be called as less fortunate people
&
It is also dedicated to the Almighty Allah, Prophet Mohammad (SM), Freedom Fighters of Bangladesh, Bangabandhu Sheikh Mujibur Rahman, Sheikh Hasina, Begum Rokeya, Kazi Nazrul Islam my parents, friends, classmates, teachers and upcoming new generations of the world.

CONTENTS

	Acknowledgments	i
1	Introduction	1
2	Notions of Egalitarian Society	5
3	Dream versus Reality of Making Egalitarian Society in Bangladesh	7
4	Conclusion	19

ACKNOWLEDGMENTS

I would like to show my sincere gratitude to Md. Pizuar Hossain, Senior Lecturer of Department of Law, East West University for his nonstop support, advice, effort, patience and important suggestions throughout the research work of my book. My supervisor started his tremendous support to complete the entire book which I will never forget. Beside my supervisor, I am grateful to the Department of Law for giving me such an opportunity to spread my knowledge. I would like to thank the Almighty Allah, my parents and all other people of the world who have supported me throughout the journey of life.

1 INTRODUCTION

'Law exists for man and not man for law and that the rules must be so adapted that injustice is avoided'[1]. This statement signifies that law is to be made in such way by which it deems that it is made for the people and it has to be with the effective force which will ensure the proper justice in every sphere of our life where the law is needed. So, it denotes that law has *'an object' and a 'purpose'* to protect the interests of the people and society[2]. According to the Pounds classification, under the purview of jurisprudence who classified the interests as for people, society and individuals because there is the presence of a well relationship between individual interests and social interests when the matter of welfare comes to play its role[3].

---

[1] Cf. *In the Matter of Davy*, [1935] P. 1, where the court refused to apply a technicality when it would have defeated the plain intention of a statute, and *Raybould Pty. Ltd. v. Dodgshum*, [1953] V.L.R. 84. Cited in G.W. Paton and David P. Derham, *A Text Book of Jurisprudence* (Oxford University Press, 4th edn, 1946) 60.

[2] A balanced survey will be found in *The Jurisprudence of Interests*, trans. M. Schoch, which contains excerpts from the writings of M. Rumelin, P. Heck, P. Oert-mann, H. Stoll, J. Binder, and H. Isay. An excellent review is E. J. Cohn, 13 *Mod. L. R.* (1950), 117.

[3] 'A Survey of Social Interests', *57 Harv. L. R.* (1943), 1. For a discussion of R. Pounds Views see E. W. Patterson in *Interpretation of Modern Legal Philosophies* (ed. P. Sayre), 558.

Therefore, Constitution itself is a mother law which can be defined as the body of the fundamental legal principles to determine the constitution of a state. The Constitution of the People's Republic of Bangladesh is the supreme law in Bangladesh which has the presence of constitutionalism. According to the different schools of jurisprudence, a question may raise before us that what is the ultimate object, purpose and ideal end of making a law; whether to protect interest of the people, society and individual or not, that is the question of fact. Therefore, according to Austin, a law can be called as valid law when it is the command of sovereign[4]. On the other hand Pound coined "law" as such way that laws main purpose is to protect the interest of the people, society and individual, but it depends on that particular societies norms and values. Accordingly, Bangladesh as a unitary, an independent and a sovereign state[5] has the Constitution as the Supreme Law[6] which contains four ideals or spirits to fulfill the interest of the people, society and individual to make an egalitarian society which was the anticipation or will of the people of Bangladesh who laid down their life for ensuring it through proper implementations[7]. The dream of making an egalitarian society is to be ensured by implementing the principles of Nationalism, Socialism, Democracy (and Human Rights) and Secularism[8]. Therefore, the preamble of this constitution states the main philosophy (moral and legal) of making this constitution[9] and it is the source of all other laws in Bangladesh[10]. It starts with the expression "[w]e"[11] and declares the aspirations of the will of the people to make sure such kind of society where there is no presence of exploitation rather a society is to be

---

[4] Ibid, 37.

[5] The Constitution of Bangladesh, art.1.

[6] Ibid, Preamble.

[7] Ibid.

[8] Ibid.

[9] Md. Abdul Halim, *Constitution, Constitutional Law and Politics: Bangladesh Perspective: A Comparative Study of Problems of Constitutionalism in Bangladesh* (Dhaka: CCB Foundation, 8th edition, 1998) 52.

[10] The Constitution of Bangladesh, Preamble.

[11] Ibid.

created within a democratic process where the rule of law, fundamental human rights and freedom, equality and justice, political, social and economic emancipation will be ensured for the people of Bangladesh[12]. Therefore, we can assume that the first part of this constitution talks about the fundamental elements which can be identified as the spirit of this Constitution[13] and the last part talks about the secondary elements which can be identified as the details of state's structure and state's action[14]. So, the spirits are the fundamental elements of this constitution which expressed the phenomenon of making an egalitarian society where "fairness and justice" is to be established in every sphere of the people's life and where no such "discrimination, inequality or injustice" on the grounds of race, caste, sex should exist[15]. Gradually, the implementation of the dream of making an egalitarian society in Bangladesh is continuing for its visible scene. The Government of Bangladesh needs to take some initiatives to fulfill the dream in terms of separation of power[16] and the proper execution of the fundamental human rights and freedom[17] which must exist in real scenario. Because, it was the vital spirit of the Proclamation of Independence[18], Declaration of Independence[19] and the Historic Speech of the Father of the Nation by Sheikh Mujibur Rahman on the 7th March, 1971[20]. He expressed the feelings of the general people to the people of Bangladesh[21] again at the inaugural session of the first meeting of the Constituent Assembly that '[o]ur people have paid with their blood for our

---

[12] Ibid.

[13] Ibid, art. 7B.

[14] The Constitution of Bangladesh.

[15] Ibid, Part II and Part III.

[16] Ibid, arts. 22, 59(1)(2), 60.

[17] Ibid, art. 11.

[18] Ibid, art. 150 (2), 7th Schedule.

[19] Ibid, art. 150 (2), 6th Schedule.

[20] Ibid, art. 150 (2), 5th Schedule.

[21] Ibid.

independence and for our right to meet today as the sovereign Constituent Assembly for Bangladesh. It is for us to ensure that the sacrifices of our martyrs will not have been in vain'[22].

---

[22] This quotation has been mentioned in Kamal Hossain, Bangladesh: Quest for Freedom and Justice, (The University Press Limited, 3rd edn. 2013) 138.

2 NOTIONS OF EGALITARIAN SOCIETY

It is to be noted that '[t]he term *'egality'*, from which *'egalitarian'* is derived, was introduced into English with its present meaning in a poem by Tennyson in 1864 to suggest politically assertive equality of the French variety'[23]. In relation to this, James Woodburn coined *"egalitarian society"* as the approximation to equality which is known in any human societies on the basis of *"equality"*[24]. As Elaine Thompson in his study of "Egalitarianism in Australia" argued about egalitarianism that it is as like a set of beliefs and is an ideology which has been built up over time and spread into the popular culture and he provided Australia as for example that it is a classless society because the income and wealth are distributed in the manner by which everyone can own their home where the rich and poor are staying in the same foot, and he took *"egalitarianism"* as an ideology because it has a core relationship with *"equality or equality of opportunity"*[25]. On the other hand, John Hirst focused in an essay on "Australian Egalitarianism" that the inequalities are developed when the "equality of opportunity is the ideal"[26]. Therefore, it seems that *"inequality"* is the term which is opposed to the *"equality"*. In the discussion on "New thinking on Egalitarianism", Robert M. Whaples noted from the Jewish-Christian perspective that *"inequality"* is the symptom of *"injustice"* and God stands against it[27]. Moreover, he took the historians point of view that *"inequality"* is nothing but a power by which a minor group can dominate the group of majority on the basis of group, sex, race, caste, religion *etc.* and they maintain the power on the subject matter of social, political and economic contexts[28].

---

[23] James Woodburn, *'Egalitarian Societies'*, September 1982, 431,431.

[24] Ibid.

[25] Thompson, *Fair Enough: Egalitarianism in Australia* (University of New South Wales Press, Sydney 1994) 266.

[26] Hirst, "Egalitarianism" (1986) 5 *Australian Cultural History* 12.

[27] Robert M. Waples,? *'Egalitarianism: Fair and Equal New Thinking on Egalitarianism'* [2017] 5, 13.

Hence, it means that the powerful minority group actually tries to curtail the human rights of the people by which they can easily deprive them on these bases. Therefore, Allah declared in Qur'an that all men are equal and they are the children of Adam (49:13) and their distinction is to be recognized only by their piety and good acts[29]. Louise Marlow found that the "Islamic ideals of egalitarianism" is the notion of *"social justice"* and *"social service"* which is alleviating suffering and helping the needy people[30]. Consequently, *"egalitarianism"* as a doctrine of the political philosophy which denotes the norms of a *"just and fair society"* where everyone is *"equal"* and continuing their life with *"human dignity"* and where no such *"exploitation"* and *"discrimination"* are present on the basis of race, sex, caste, religion or ethnicity. Moreover, from the social, political and economic perspective, the society needs to be established in such manner where there is no chance of the presence of *"inequality or injustice"* which is the opposite term of *"equality"* as the base of *"egalitarian society"*.

---

[28] Ibid, 10.

[29] Poonwala, Ismail k, *Iranian Studies* (1999) 32(3) 405,405.

[30] Ibid.

3 DREAMS VERSUS REALITY OF MAKING EGALITARIAN SOCIETY IN BANGLADESH

The constitution of Bangladesh is achieved through a historic liberation war of independence and that is why it was made by the framers in different way from others' constitution[31]. In this constitution the people's feature is to be deemed as "dominant actors" and therefore, the manifestation of it is called as the "people's power"[32]. Article 1 of the Constitution of Bangladesh declares that Bangladesh is a unitary, independent and sovereign "Republic" which is to be known as the "People's Republic of Bangladesh". Here, the term "Republic" is again emphasized and it means that this state is to be run with the elected functionary system rather than the system of monarchy[33]. Article 7 expresses with the greatest phenomenon of "Lives"[34] who laid down their majestic life for the "Independence of Bangladesh"[35] that in the "republic" all powers belong to the "people" and this "Constitution" is the "solemn expression" of the "will of the people"[36] and it is the "supreme law" of the "republic". Besides, the framers of the Constitution of Bangladesh realized the necessity of the preamble which can speak about the norms of making this Constitution and its ultimate object to make sure a picture of an "egalitarian society" in Bangladesh to protect the "will of the people"[37]. Because, it was the aspiration of the "brave martyrs of Bangladesh" and that is why the

---

[31] *Dr. Mohiuddin Farooque v. Bangladesh*, (1997) 49 DLR (AD) 1, Para 41.

[32] Mahmudul Islam, *Constitutional Law of Bangladesh* (Bangladesh: Mullick Brothers, 3rd edn. 2016) 19.

[33] Ibid.

[34] The Constitution of Bangladesh, Preamble.

[35] Ibid.

[36] Ibid.

[37] Ibid, art. 6.

preamble contains the vital norms to reach the dream of making an "egalitarian society" in "Bangalee culture". Therefore, Lamer CJ of Canada considered the preamble as 'the grand entrance hall to the castle of the constitution'[38]. For that reason, "preamble" is the normative part of the Constitution of Bangladesh[39] which shall not be used to change or modify the language of the Constitution[40], but it can be used as an aid for the interpretation of the intention of the framers when any provision of the Constitution runs counter to the spirit and objectives as stated in the preamble[41], or when the language of the Constitution is not clear or ambiguous[42].

Now, if we look at the norms of the preamble then it speaks about the four high ideals such as Nationalism, Socialism, Democracy and Secularism which shall be the fundamental principles of the constitution of Bangladesh. With the accumulation of these principles there shall be a fundamental aim of the state to realize it through the "democratic process a socialist society" which is free from all sorts of "exploitation" and "discrimination"[43]. In that particular society the rule of law, fundamental human rights, freedom, equality and justice as per the political, social and economic goal will be secured for all citizens. Moreover, the preamble talks about the will of the people and the will is to be deemed as the prosperity in freedom and co-operation in keeping with the progressive aspirations of mankind which is the norms of an egalitarian society that everyone is equal. Accordingly, art.27 states that in this state all citizens are equal before law and they are entitled to get the equal protection of law[44], and art.28 emphasizes that the state shall not discriminate any citizen on the grounds of race, caste, sex or place of birth. Moreover, it emphasized that the women have equal rights like the men in all spheres of the state and public

---

[38] *Reference re Provincial Court Judges,* [1997] 3 SCR 3.

[39] *Anwar Hossain Chowdhury v. Bangladesh,* 1989 BLD (Spl) 1.

[40] Ibid.

[41] Mahmudul Islam, *Constitutional Law of Bangladesh* (Dhaka: Mullick Brothers, 3rd edn. 2016) 66.

[42] *A.G. v Prince Earnest Augustus,* 1057 AC 436, 467-68.

[43] The Constitution of Bangladesh, Preamble.

[44] Ibid, Part III.

life under the equal protection of law of the state[45]. It is further stated in art. 28 (4) that nothing in this article shall prevent the state from making special provision in favor of women and child or for the advancement of any backward section of citizens[46].

Art. 31 talks about right to protection of law which is an inalienable right of every citizen of Bangladesh, where no sorts of particular action detrimental to the life, liberty, body and reputation or property of any citizen shall be taken[47]. Besides, the framers of the constitution of Bangladesh through art.32 provided their supreme care by incorporating the fundamental right that is the protection of "right to life" and "personal liberty"[48]. Moreover, this fundamental right again placed in art.33 and 35 for the safeguard in case of arrest, detention and in respect of trial and punishment[49]. For making an egalitarian society, the Constitution of Bangladesh prohibited the child labor and forced labor in art. 34 except for criminal offence or required by law for public purposes[50]. Besides, there are some rights of human being like freedom of movement, assembly and association incorporated in arts.36, 37 and 38 with reasonable restrictions[51].

Whereas, only art.39 (1) declared that freedom of thought and conscience is granted and it is to be deemed as absolute right of a person[52]. Even though it is the obligation of the state to ensure that every citizen has the right to profess, practice or propagate his/her religion and they have the right in respect of their religious community to make their institutions abide by the laws of Bangladesh[53]. Moreover, every citizen has the right to

---

[45] Ibid.

[46] Ibid.

[47] Ibid.

[48] Ibid.

[49] Ibid.

[50] Ibid.

[51] Ibid.

[52] Ibid.

[53] Ibid.

acquire, hold, transfer, or otherwise can dispose it and at the same time, they have the fundamental right of getting the protection of privacy and other means of communication[54]. At last, art.44 of the Constitution of Bangladesh defines the way of the enforceability of these fundamental rights and accordingly, every citizen has the right to move to the High Court Division for the enforcement of the fundamental rights which are guaranteed by this Part III of the Constitution of Bangladesh. Therefore, according to the art.94, 100, and 102 High Court Division established where all the Judges are independent in the all functions of it who has the constitutional and original jurisdiction also[55]. Basically, the power is given to them by the constitution of Bangladesh to protect the fundamental rights of its citizen who aggrieved. This mechanism made by the framers because the dream of making an egalitarian society was the anticipation of those people who laid down their life in 1971 to make sure such a society which is free from exploitation, discrimination and injustice.

---

[54] Ibid, arts.42 and 43.

[55] Ibid, Part VI.

[A] Factors that Lead to Make an Egalitarian Society in Bangladesh

In the *Kudrat-E-Elahi v. Bangladesh*[56] case, M. Kamal J pointed out that the fundamental principles of the Constitution of Bangladesh can be distinguished from the laws where there is no applicability of art. 7 though it talks about the perspective of the supremacy of the constitution. For that reason, S. Ahmed CJ stated that:

'[t]hey are in the nature of People's programme for socio-economic development of the country in peaceful manner, not overnight, but gradually. Implementation of these programmes; require resources, technical know-how and many other things including mass-education. Whether all these pre-requisites for a peaceful socio-economic revolution exist is for the state to decide'[57].

Art.16 placed for removing the disparity in the standards of living between the urban and rural areas, and for that reason the state shall adopt such kind of effective measures which can bring a radical transformation in the rural areas through the promotion of an agricultural revolution, rural electrification, development of cottage and other industries with the improvement of proper education, communications and public health[58]. Accordingly, art.17 talks about the notion of extending free and compulsory education for all the children, and that is why the state shall adopt effective measures to establish a uniform, mass- oriented and universal system of education policy because the state admits to remove the illiteracy from the society within a certain period of time[59]. Moreover, art.15 (a) states the basic necessities of life including food, clothing, shelter, education and medical care. In the same article, clause (b) talks about the right to work at a reasonable wage having regard to the proper quality and quantity of work[60].

---

[56] (1992) 44DLR (AD) 319.

[57] Ibid, p.331.

[58] The Constitution of Bangladesh.

[59] *Ain-0-Salish Kendra v. Bangladesh,* (2011) 63 DLR 95.

[60] The Constitution of Bangladesh.

With a view to securing to its citizens art.15 (c) (d) further states that right to reasonable rest, recreation, leisure and social security in case of unemployment crisis, illness, disablement, old age, orphans or widows has to be ensured by the state[61]. Moreover, art. 15(a) states about the provision of basic necessities of life, including food, clothing, shelter, education and medical care; art.15 (b) states for the right to work which has guaranteed the employment at a reasonable wage having regard to the quality and quantity of work and art.15 (c)(d) talks about the right to reasonable rest, recreation, leisure and social security in the case of unemployment crisis, illness, disablement, old age, orphans or suffered by widows[62]. So, these are the fundamental responsibilities of Bangladesh as a state which has to attain through a planned economic growth to secure its citizens for increasing the productive forces and improving the material and cultural standard of living of the people.

Art.19 talks about the "equality of opportunity" where it denotes that the state shall take such kind of effective measures by which it is ensured that all citizens are getting the equal opportunity to remove social and economic inequality between the people of this state to ensure a equitable society through the equitable distribution of wealth to the citizens, and also declared that the economic development throughout the "Republic" shall attain a uniform level where the state shall ensure the equal opportunity of the women in case of their participation in all spheres of their national life as much as possible[63]. Therefore, art.20 mentions in the Constitution of Bangladesh that work is a right and it is a duty and matter of honor for all the citizens of Bangladesh who are capable to work, but they will be paid for their work on the basis of a principle which took its right position in the Constitution of Bangladesh that "from each according to his abilities and to each according to his work"[64]. It is included here because the Constitution of Bangladesh has no place for injustice or inequality and the state shall endeavor to ensure equality which is opposed of the former term by which no person shall able to enjoy any income which is unearned rather than any person can enjoy their earned incomes if it was made by their human labor in every form or intellectual or physical labor which shall become a fuller

---

[61] Ibid.

[62] Ibid.

[63] The Constitution of Bangladesh.

[64] Ibid, art. 20.

expression of the human dignity and creative endeavor of the human personality[65].

Moreover, art.14 illustrates that it shall be the fundamental responsibility of the state to emancipate the toiling masses, peasants, workers and the backward sections from all forms of exploitation because the state admit it in the fundamental principle of state policy and the "economic emancipation"[66] was the anticipation of the framers of this Constitution. Hence, the Constitution of Bangladesh clearly indicates that the state is not based on the basis of a communist or such a socialist philosophy where the wealth is to be staying only under the authority of state and the wealth is to be redistributed to among the people under the authority of state[67] rather all powers belong to the people[68]. Besides, the exercise of powers of the people is to be enforceable through their effective participation where the ultimate "choice" of them is to be highly counted with their human dignity to the national interest of Bangladesh[69] to establish an "egalitarian society"[70] within the aim of the four ideals of the Constitution of Bangladesh[71]. For that reason, the principle of nationalism has been invoked in this constitution for identifying the unity, solidarity, sovereignty and independence of this country[72]. The principles of socialism and secularism has been invoked for establishing a socialist economic system to attain a just and an egalitarian society which will be free from all sorts of exploitation which exploitation of man can be made by man[73] and on the basis of religion no sorts of exploitation and discrimination[74] will exist in

---

[65] Ibid.

[66] Ibid, art. 10.

[67] Islam (n 41).

[68] The Constitution of Bangladesh, art.7.

[69] Ibid, art. 11.

[70] Ibid, art. 10.

[71] Ibid, arts. 9, 10, 11, 12.

[72] Ibid, arts. 1, 2.

[73] Ibid, art. 10.

the perspective of social, economic and political point of view[75]. Lastly, the principle of democracy invoked for ensuring the human rights, freedom, dignity and the effective participation of them to choose their elected representatives by whom they want to carry on their all governmental and non-governmental administrative functions in Bangladesh[76]. Therefore, art.8 talks about the fundamental principles of state policy and the above mentioned four principles are to be deemed as the fundamental "spirits" to govern the state[77].

These shall be applied for making the laws of Bangladesh and, shall be used as a guide for the interpretation of the Constitution of Bangladesh and these shall formed the basis of work of the state and its citizens[78]. At the same time, it is to be noted that these four principles shall not be judicially enforceable[79] because these are the fundamental principles of state policy[80], and it can be said that this is the limitation. However, these principles provide an obligation upon the government to act on them[81] and can set aside any law which is passed by the Parliament[82] when the Supreme Court of Bangladesh finds it as unconstitutional or inconsistent with the Constitution[83]. Therefore, only the strongest way to reach the goal of an egalitarian society which means about the unity and solidarity of Bangalee nation deriving from its language, culture, sovereignty, independency

---

[74] Ibid, art. 12.

[75] Ibid, Preamble.

[76] Ibid, art. 11.

[77] Ibid.

[78] Ibid, art. 8.

[79] Ibid, art.

[80] *Saleemullah v. Justice M.A. Quddus Chowdhury,* (1994) 46 DLR 691; *Aftabuddin v. Bangladesh,* (1996) 48 DLR 1.

[81] *Wahab v. Secretary, Ministry of Land, (1996)* 1 MLR 338; *Major- General KM Safiullah v. Bangladesh* (2010) 18 BLT.

[82] The Constitution of Bangladesh, art. 65.

[83] Ibid, art. 7.

through a determined struggle of a liberation war in 1971 for making such a just socialist society. The society must be free from the exploitation of man by man which is possible if the utmost power of people's choice of electing someone as his or her representative and the person as a representative always represent the citizen because he or she has chosen him or her for representing themselves[84].

---

[84] Ibid, art.9, 10, 11,12 and 66.

[B] Selected Challenges to Ensure Complete Egalitarian Society in Bangladesh

The term discrimination, deprivation and exploitation come when no such equality and justice is present in a society. In 1971, the peoples of Bangladesh laid down their valuable lives for making such kind of a society which will be free from inequality and injustice[85]. Though their anticipation placed in the written constitution of Bangladesh[86], but it is the matter of sorrow that inequality and injustice is going on within our society on the basis of race, sex, caste, religion and ethnicity. This was not the dream of making an egalitarian society. If we look at the intention of the framers through the subjective phenomenon of the preamble then a vital question may raise before us that whether the previous and present government of Bangladesh came out from the terms of the exploitation and discrimination or not or whether fairness is to be ensured or not that is the question of fact. But it was and is the responsibility and accountability with mandatory obligation under the constitution of Bangladesh upon the government of it[87].

Now if we try to observe the annual report 2017 of Ain-o-Salish-Kendra then we can see that the violence against women and child is continuing in our society. According to this report within 2017, more than 1919 women and 1055 child faced different sorts of violence[88]. Among them 620 women killed for such violence and 11 committed suicide[89]. Besides, 818 women and girl raped, among them 7 died. Moreover 442 women harassed for the domestic violence and sexually harassed 170. Because of dowry relating issues 145 women killed[90]. Therefore, it is a challenge for the government of Bangladesh to protect the women and child from any sorts of exploitation like violence, rape, torture or physical sufferings or mental agony which constitutes the violence of human dignity. According to the

---

[85] Ibid, Preamble.

[86] Ibid.

[87] The Constitution of Bangladesh, Preamble.

[88] Ibid.

[89] Ibid.

[90] Ibid.

judgment of *Bangladesh Mahila Ainjibi Samity vs. Ministry of Home Affairs*[91], security of life is a right to life.

In 2017, the Government of Bangladesh finalized a draft of "*Sastho Seba Ain* 2017" or "Health Care Act, 2017" for ensuring better health care services to the people of this State where section 25 of the same Act provides an indemnity to the doctors. Though a female student of University of Dhaka named Afifa Choity died on 18 May 2017 at the central Hospital in Dhaka for the doctor's wrong treatment. It is the matter of sorrow that though a case was filed against the doctors including the Director of that hospital, but it was withdrawn by the family of that victim through under pressure[92].

In another case, Parvin Akter who gave birth to a child on the street before the "Matrisadan o Sishu Shastya Proshikshan Protishthan" on 17 October 2017 was denied to get the basic care from three governmental hospitals. For that reason, the new born child of this nation died after the birth[93]. So that life, liberty, body, reputation and property curtailed for the lack of proper protection and implementation of law. But these are the subject matter of the fundamental rights of the people of Bangladesh.

In another case, the same thing emphasized by the judgment of *Dr.Mohiuddin Faruquee vs. Bangladesh*[94] that right to life includes the protection of health, normal longevity, life protection and improvement of environment. In case of women, the right to life and liberty includes the right to work with their own dignity which is free from any form of sexual harassment. Therefore, in the case of *Salma Ali vs. Bangladesh*[95] and *Blast Vs Bangladesh*[96] it was the findings that it is the constitutional obligation for the government of Bangladesh to enact proper laws to protect the women and girls at their workplaces, duties and also from their educational institutions in according to their fundamental rights.

---

[91] 2008 BLD 580.

[92] Please visit, http://www.askbd.org/ask/2019/03/13/annual-report-2017-ask/.

[93] Ibid, page. 17.

[94] (1996) 48 DLR 438.

[95] 2009 BLD 415.

[96] (2011) 63 DLR 1.

Now if we look at the poorest persons or slummy people or homeless or illiterate people and the child of them then can see that they are surviving for economical ability, shelter, food, health safety and the recreation. Therefore, they are not competing able with the middle class or upper class societies who are staying at the dominating position as dominators. So, they are depriving and discriminating, though it is the constitutional obligation upon the government to ensure the economical emancipation among the people[97]. But fortunately or unfortunately Bangladesh is staying far away from that picture. Now the question may raise that whether they are living or surviving that is another question of fact. In Dhaka city 90 wards exist within 215.04 sq. kms, where more than 3500 slum dwellers present[98]. There more than 45 lakh slummy people are living and among them 70% adults are illiterate[99]. According to the article 27, 28, 29, 31, 32, 34, 37, 38, 39, 40 and 41 they are clearly depriving from their 'fundamental rights' and also 'right to life' which are guaranteed by the constitution of Bangladesh. Moreover, art. 11, 14, 15, 16, 17, 18, 19 and 20 emphasized for ensuring compulsory primary education for the children by adopting special measures as well as for them who are physically and mentally under challenged[100]. But, because of the economic impoverishment, socio-economic adversity, social insecurity and unemployment of their guardian they are depriving from their rights. In this modern time, the rootless people and their child has to take shelter either in a slum or any other places under the sky where there is nothing would to say that it is mine.

Therefore, in the divine mind of their child no question is to be raised that whether there is any security of mine or not. But art.31 includes the "human dignity" and "decency" and the right to get general necessities of life as like the basic foods, cloths, shelters along with some facilities which as a general human being need to live in a society[101]. But it is the commitment of the constitution of Bangladesh to its citizen that everyone in this sovereign State shall be protected by the equal protection of law and

---

[97] The Constitution of Bangladesh, art. 10

[98] Dr. Mizanur Rahman, *Human Rights and Corruption* (Dhaka: Empowerment through Law of the Common People, 1st edn. 2007) 186.

[99] Ibid.

[100] The Constitution of Bangladesh.

[101] Ibid.

proper security will be furnished according the law[102]. Now it comes to the eyes of these people who are the main source of national power that all citizens are equal before law who are entitled to get the equal protection of law should not be just written down in a paper of book. Rather the government has to ensure a just and true egalitarian society in Bangladesh through establishing equality and this was the aspirations of the freedom fighter. Besides, art.7 of the constitution of expressed that the people is the main source of power of this sovereign State and the exercise of their power shall be affected only under and by the authority of the constitution[103]. Further, art.7 (2) emphasized that this constitution should be deemed as the solemn expression of the will of the people. Now the question may raise that whether the certain class of people of Bangladesh is to be deemed as the people of Bangladesh or the mass people of this nation would be deemed as the people of Bangladesh as per the will of the people, that is another question of fact. So that it is so much true that the people of Bangladesh are depriving from justice.

In another context, if we try to observe an egalitarian society then can see that on the basis of religion, caste or ethnicity no discrimination is to be present there. Moreover, equal treatment is to be ensured by the government. But unfortunately the violence against the aboriginal or minority or ethnic people or Hindu community is going on in our society. According to the annual report 2017 which was published by Ain-o-Salish-Kendra 279 number of violence happened against the Hindu and minor community[104]. Besides, 45 houses of them are destroyed and fired[105]. Therefore, where an egalitarian society is to be established in Bangladesh, but there right to life does not ensure properly. So that along with the others fundamental right if the right to life exist, only then the fairness will be visible, otherwise not.

---

[102] Ibid, Preamble.

[103] Ibid.

[104] Please visit, http://www.askbd.org/ask/2019/03/13/annual-report-2017-ask/

[105] Ibid.

4 CONCLUSIONS

Bangladesh is such kind of a state which was achieved by the liberation war in 1971 through the character of rebellion phenomenon[106]. The people of this country laid down their lives for making such kind of a country where an egalitarian society will be ensured[107]. It was the greatest dream of them. Therefore, the framers made the Constitution of Bangladesh with the accumulation of Nationalism, Socialism, Democracy and Secularism[108]. For that reason, these four principles are to be called as the heart of this constitution and these are to be deemed as the fundamental principle of the state[109]. These are also placed in the preamble for making such kind of a sense by which an egalitarian society will be ensured one day and according to these principle the government should act like that way to fulfill the dream of brave martyrs[110]. They believed to build up such a society where no sorts of the exploitation, discrimination and injustice can present[111]. Therefore, they provided such a philosophical point of view by which we can say that hope is that which never dies till the rest of its journey[112]. Therefore, if the government of Bangladesh through the effective measures can remove the exploitation, discrimination and injustice from this society, then the dream of making an egalitarian society can be visible[113].

---

[106] The Constitution of Bangladesh, Preamble.

[107] Ibid.

[108] Ibid, art. 9, 10, 11, 12.

[109] Ibid.

[110] Ibid, Preamble.

[111] Ibid.

[112] Ibid.

[113] Ibid.

BIBLIOGRAPHY

Books and Articles
1) Halim, Md. Abdul, *Constitutional Law and Politics: Bangladesh Perspective: A Comparative Study of Problems of Constitutionalism in Bangladesh* (Dhaka: CCB Foundation, 8th edn, 1998).
2) Hirst, "*Egalitarianism*" (1986) 5 Australian Cultural History 12.
3) Hossain, Kamal, Bangladesh: *Quest for freedom and Justice*, (The University Press Limited, 3rd edn. 2013).
4) Islam, Mahmudul, *Constitutional Law of Bangladesh* (Dhaka: Mullick Brothers, 3rd edn. 2016).
5) Ismail, K. Poonwala, *Iranian Studies* (1999) 32(3) 405.
6) James, Woodburn, '*Egalitarian Societies*', September, 1982, 431.
7) Paton, G.W. and Derham David P., *A Text Book of Jurisprudence* (Oxford University Press, 4th edn, 1946).
8) Patterson, E. W., *Interpretation of Modern Legal Philosophies* (ed. P. Sayre), 558.
9) Rahman, Dr. Mizanur, *Human Rights and corruption* (Dhaka: Empowerment through Law of the Common People, 1st edn. 2007).
10) Thompson, *Fair Enough: Egalitarianism in Australia* (University of New South Wales Press, Sydney 1994).
11) Waples, Robert M., '*Egalitarianism: Fair and Equal New Thinking on Egalitarianism*' [2017] 5.

Cases
1) *G. v Prince Earnest Augustus*, 1057 AC 436, 467-68.
2) *Aftabuddin v. Bangladesh*, (1996) 48 DLR 1.
3) *Ain-O-Salish Kendra v. Bangladesh*, (2011) 63 DLR 95.
4) *Anwar Hossain Chowdhury v. Bangladesh*, 1989 BLD (Spl) 1.
5) *Bangladesh Jatiya Mahila Ainjibi Samity v. Ministry of Home Affairs*, 2008 BLD 580.
6) *Blast v. Bangladesh*, (2011) 63 DLR 1.
7) *D.K Basu v. W.B.*, AIR 1997 SC 610.
8) *Dr. Mohiuddin Farooque v. Bangladesh*, (1996) 48 DLR 438.
9) *Gautam v. Subhra Chakraborty*, AIR 1996 SC 922.
10) *Kudrat-E-Elahi v. Bangladesh* (1992) 44 DLR (AD) 319.
11) *Major- General KM Safiullah v. Bangladesh* (2010) 18 BLT.
12) *Olga Tellis v. Bombay Municipal Crop*. AIR 1986 SC 180.

13) *Rayboulds Pty. Ltd. v. Dodgshum*, [1953] V.L.R 84.
14) *Saleemullah v. Justice M.A Quddus Chowdhury*, (1994) 46 DLR 691.
15) *Salma Ali v.Bangladesh*, 2009 BLD 415.
16) *Sube Singh v. Haryana*, AIR 2006 SC 1117.
17) *Wahab v. Secretary, Ministry of Land*, (1996) 1 MLR 338.

ABOUT THE AUTHOR

MD. SAD BIN ABI is the son of Md. Sakhawat Hossain and Mst. Azifa Anjumanara Begum, married to Mst. Naziba Tahsin Soumik is a student of the Department of Law, East West University, and Dhaka, Bangladesh.

He has born at 1997 in a rural area of Bangladesh. He completed the Secondary and Higher Secondary study from Cantonment Public School and College, located at Parbatipur, Dinajpur. Afterwards he came to Dhaka for completing the higher study and admitted into the Department of Law, East West University. It was the anticipation of him to go ahead with human dignity to do something for the less-fortunate people all over the world and accordingly he is writing for the whole people of this planet.

He scored CGPA. 3.68 (out of 4) (First class result) from East West University and completed his bachelor degree (LL.B Hon's) as a Dean's Listed student. Besides, He achieved the Merit Scholarship Certificate and Medha Lalon Scholarship from the same university.

Mailing Address: B-Block, Road # 04, Banasree, Rampura, Dhaka-1219
Contact: 01766395097
Email: aanupom92@gmail.com

www.ingramcontent.com/pod-product-compliance
Lightning Source LLC
Chambersburg PA
CBHW040301220526
45473CB00002B/550